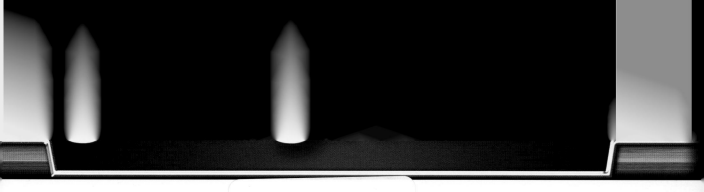

Lotus

Tracy Nelson Maurer

Rourke
Publishing LLC
Vero Beach, Florida 32964

www.rourkepublishing.com

We recognize that some words, model names and designations, for example, mentioned herein are the property of the trademark holder. We use them for identification purposes only. This is not an official publication.

PHOTO CREDITS: Courtesy of Group Lotus PLC

AUTHOR CREDITS:
The author gratefully acknowledges project assistance provided by Alistair Florance at Lotus Cars Ltd., Kit Bolton at Minneapolis Downtown Jaguar/Lotus, Phil Ethier, Tim Engel, and Terry Pitts.

Also, the author extends appreciation to Mike Maurer, Lois M. Nelson, Margaret and Thomas, and the team at Rourke.

Editor: Robert Stengard-Olliges
Cover Design: Todd Field
Page Design: Nicola Stratford

Library of Congress Cataloging-in-Publication Data

Maurer, Tracy, 1965-
  Lotus / Tracy Nelson Maurer.
    p. cm. -- (Full throttle)
  Includes index.
  ISBN 1-60044-226-9 (hardcover)
  ISBN 978-1-60044-366-4 (paperback)
  1. Lotus automobiles--Juvenile literature. I. Title. II. Series: Maurer, Tracy, 1965-. Full throttle.

  TL215.L67M38 2006
  629.222'2--dc22

                              2006017499

Printed in the USA

CG/CG

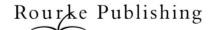

Rourke Publishing

www.rourkepublishing.com – sales@rourkepublishing.com
Post Office Box 3328, Vero Beach, FL 32964

Table of Contents

The Clever Company

Cleverly designed Lotus cars have won fans—and races—all over the world. The British company's founder, Colin Chapman, built the Lotus Mark I in 1948 at age 20. He soon discovered racing and tinkered with more and more car designs to reach lower vehicle weights.

Fast Fact

Caterham Cars still builds
the Lotus Seven design, now
called the Caterham Seven.

Anthony Colin Bruce Chapman

Anthony Colin Bruce Chapman (1928-1982)
grew up in England. He flew airplanes for the
Royal Air Force before starting Lotus
Engineering Company in 1952.

Chapman numbered his racecar designs,
starting with the Lotus Mark 1. His system had
a few quirks. He designed the Mark V but
didn't produce it. And, some collectors say he
skipped unlucky 13. He followed the Twelve
with the Eleven Series 2.

Built out of order
(after the Mark VI and
eight additional models),
the 1957 Lotus Seven was
the world's first **kit car**.
Lotus sold customers a
box of parts instead of a
drivable car.

5

Rolling Out Firsts

Chapman branched off from racecars with the Type 14 Elite road car in 1957. The new two-seater design featured the world's first **fiberglass monocoque** car—one of many firsts for Lotus. The load-bearing shell improved the car's handling and lowered its weight. The idea came from airplanes, something Chapman knew a lot about.

*The Lotus Europa was one of the first production road cars with an engine mounted near the middle to power its **rear-wheel drive** system. Lotus made them from 1966 to 1975.*

fiberglass
glass strands woven into plastic for added strength

monocoque
in vehicles, a body constructed with the frame as a single unit

rear-wheel drive
the engine drives the rear wheels, pushing the vehicle forward

Chapman's design for the Elite inspired monocoque Formula 1 racecars.

Clever Ideas

Lotus has proven many new design ideas:

- Building a car using a frameless fiberglass load-bearing shell
- Producing rear-wheel drive, mid-engine road cars
- Developing active suspension systems
- Inventing in-car noise-canceling systems
- Creating bonded extruded-aluminum chassis production
- Designing seats for better driver blood flow

Wild Wedges

The exotic wedge design of the Lotus Esprit fit James Bond perfectly for the 1977 movie, *The Spy Who Loved Me*. Lotus rarely made more than 500 Esprits each year, for a total of about 10,675 from 1976 to 2004.

The James Bond Lotus turned into a submarine in the movie *The Spy Who Loved Me*. Collectors prize the finned cars used in the water scenes.

Powered with a **V-8** engine after 1987, the Lotus Esprit hit 0 to 60 miles (97 km) per hour in less than 4.5 seconds and blasted from 0 to 100 miles (160 km) per hour in under 11 seconds.

Chapman died suddenly in 1982 and his company sank into money troubles. Several businesses took a turn owning Lotus, including carmakers General Motors and Bugatti. Another carmaker, Proton Holdings of Malaysia, bought Lotus in 1996. Even with so many owners, the classic Lotus badge still recalls the founder's initials and the company's clever heritage.

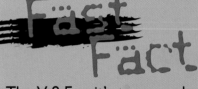

The V-8 Esprit's top speed was 175 mph (282 km/h).

Glory Days Again

Many Lotus road cars gained fame for squeezing massive power from small, four-cylinder engines. Hoping to restore the firm's glory in the 1990s, Lotus shifted back to Colin Chapman's quest for lean, fast, and stylish machines. It worked. Lotus unveiled the lightweight and snappy Elise in 1995. The new design revved up sales like no other Lotus car before it.

*Riding on the world's first non-welded **extruded-aluminum chassis**, the Elise weighs just 1,984 pounds (900 kg)—about half of a typical car.*

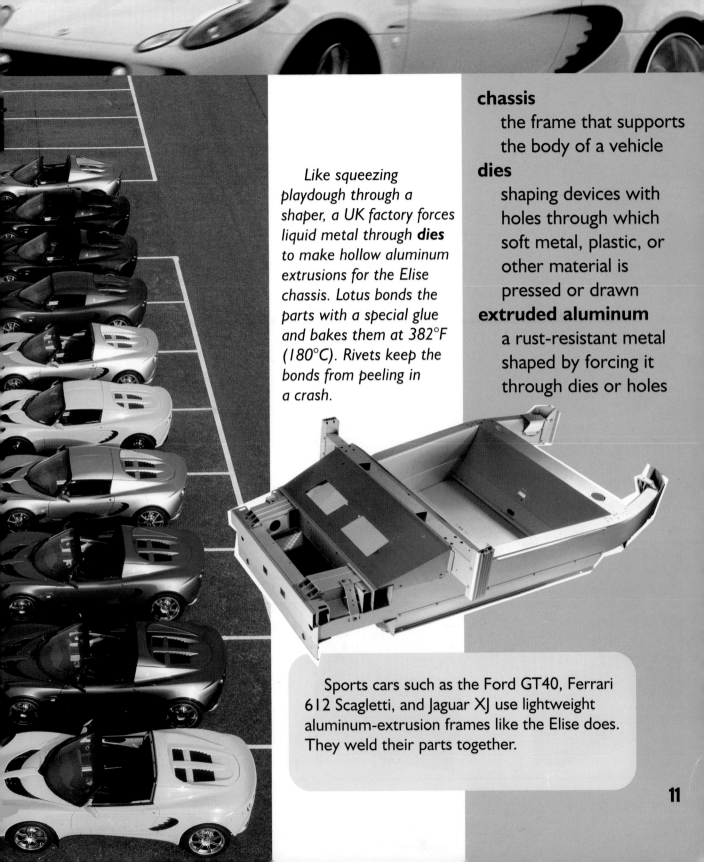

chassis
　the frame that supports the body of a vehicle

dies
　shaping devices with holes through which soft metal, plastic, or other material is pressed or drawn

extruded aluminum
　a rust-resistant metal shaped by forcing it through dies or holes

*Like squeezing playdough through a shaper, a UK factory forces liquid metal through **dies** to make hollow aluminum extrusions for the Elise chassis. Lotus bonds the parts with a special glue and bakes them at 382°F (180°C). Rivets keep the bonds from peeling in a crash.*

Sports cars such as the Ford GT40, Ferrari 612 Scagletti, and Jaguar XJ use lightweight aluminum-extrusion frames like the Elise does. They weld their parts together.

In 1958, Lotus started naming its road cars with the letter E: Elite, Éclat, Excel, Élan, Europa, Esprit, Elise, and Exige.

Carmaker Bugatti owned Lotus at the start of the project code-named 111. One-Eleven S (S for Sprint) nearly became the car's name until Bugatti boss Romano Artiloli named the new car "Elise" after his granddaughter.

The Exige is the Elise's more **aerodynamic** twin.

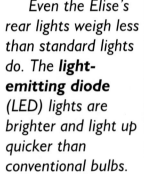

Even the Elise's rear lights weigh less than standard lights do. The **light-emitting diode** (LED) lights are brighter and light up quicker than conventional bulbs.

aerodynamic
air flows easily over the body for greater speed
light-emitting diode
a tiny electronic device that sends out light when energy flows through it

The Exige interior is black, which easily matches all 20 exterior colors.

Building Cars by Hand

In 1966, Chapman settled Lotus Engineering Company northeast of London in Hethel at a former U.S. air base. Today, Group Lotus houses both Lotus Cars and Lotus Engineering divisions at the Hethel headquarters. Designing, manufacturing, research and development, and sales planning happen there.

Factory tours show off the body bonding, painting, chassis assembly, final assembly, and quality checking areas. People from all over the world come to see how Lotus builds cars.

A "build sheet" tells Lotus workers how to make each Elise. The process takes about 10 days to finish a car. Lotus hand-builds about 4,500 cars each year at the Hethel location.

More than 70,000 Lotus cars have rolled out since Chapman's first vehicle. About 20,000 of those cars sold in the last 10 years, thanks to the Elise and Exige.

Fast Fact

Lotus makes the gear shifter for the six-speed manual transmission. It does not make all of the car parts.

Layers of Paint

For the Elise, painting takes the most factory time. Fresh fiberglass is too smooth to hold paint. Workers must first sand the panels for a rougher surface. Then they apply two layers of **primer**, two layers of paint, and two layers of gloss. Each layer bakes for at least 40 minutes. The painted parts are started early so they're ready for the chassis.

Some manufacturers paint several car bodies one color before grouping another set for a different color. At Lotus, every car is painted and assembled one at a time.

Lotus focuses on quality. Years ago, the company tested finished cars on the track. Now it uses a computer called a **dynamometer**, or dyno, to catch problems.

A trip through the rain garage reveals leaks before the customer ever sits in the car.

dynamometer
a tool for measuring a vehicle's power
primer
a base paint that seals the surface

Engine Expertise

Lotus coaxes extreme performance from its cars—usually without building its own engines. Companies such as Ford, Toyota, Renault, Isuzu, and Rover have supplied motors for Lotus. Lotus tweaks the engines to gain **horsepower** and **torque**.

Performance Factors

When Lotus designs a car, the engineers think about many factors that can help improve the vehicle's performance.

Low weight	Forget unnecessary luxury features like heated seats.
Air intake	Use scoops to drive air into the cylinders for better combustion.
Low weight	Slim down fat parts. Use fewer parts to do more work.
Aerodynamics	Shape the car to cut air like a hot knife slicing butter, but keep pressure on the car to hug the road.
Low weight	Hack off more fat. Less weight improves speed and handling.
Balance	Set the engine and distribute the weight for quick power transfer and handling.
Low weight	Just can't say it enough!

horsepower
    a measure of mechanical power

torque
    a measure of mechanical strength or force produced by an engine

Fast Fact

The Elise uses four cylinders positioned in a straight line, not in a V.

The Elise zips from 0 to 60 miles (97 km) per hour in under five seconds. But unlike beefy competitors, the speedy Elise taps a mere 1.8-liter, 4-cylinder engine to crank out 190 horsepower.

Sensible Jaw-Dropping Style

Lotus cars sport jaw-dropping style for practical reasons, such as aerodynamics. *Sensible-shmensible!* Any Lotus stops traffic. Experienced Lotus owners often warn new owners to expect questions from curious gawkers, invitations to race, and radar scans from patrols.

Huge swooping hood ducts and curvy side-body air scoops put exclamation points on the Elise's design. But they're not just for looks. They help improve performance.

Julian Thompson

Julian Thompson designed the Elise. The Ferrari Dino GT, Ducati motorcycle, and the original Ford GT40 influenced his design.

The Europa

After the Exige, Lotus revisited the Europa. Designers borrowed the Elise's chassis technology for the 2006 two-seater Europa S touring model. They also made the trunk bigger and added cushy luxuries.

In Great Britain, drivers travel in the left lane. In America, drivers use the right lane. Lotus moves the steering wheels to the left side of cars it sells in the U.S. The Elise chassis adapts easily to either left- or right-hand drive.

21

Car Talk

People in England speak English, but not the same way as Americans do. Some differences in automobile terms:

- *Bonnet* in England means *hood* in America.
- *Hood* in England means a *convertible's soft top* in America.
- *Boot* in England means *trunk* in America.

Lotus exports the Elise to nearly 40 countries. More than half go to the U.S.

Nicknamed the Federal Elise, the American model has more standard upgrades than the European version to meet U.S. laws for safety, pollution, and comfort.

American license plates are taller and wider than tags from most other countries. The Federal Elise has European bumpers with special plate mounts.

Lotus received the Queen's Award for Enterprise in 2002. The "e" on the back window of the Federal Elise symbolizes this high honor. Europeans see it on the side buttress.

Lotus expects to send about 350 of the Exige to the U.S. each year.

Championship Legacy

Colin Chapman never even saw a motor race before he entered his Lotus Mark II at the Silverstone Circuit in 1950. He beat out the favored Type 37 Bugatti. The upset win spurred Chapman into racecar designing. Lotus left several more "Marks" in the racing history books over the years.

Chapman's suspension ideas added control for racers and influenced Formula One (F1) racing.

Team Lotus entered Formula One (F1) races from 1958 to 1994. The Lotus racing team separated from the car-making company along the way.

Some grand prix courses follow city streets instead of oval tracks.

England's Silverstone Circuit held the very first F1 World Championship grand prix race in 1950. Europe is the home to F1 racing with many famous winding courses.

Formula One, or Grand Prix, racing attracts the world's top drivers and the most advanced (and most expensive!) single-seat, open-wheel cars. Prizes go to drivers and carmakers, called constructors.

A Clever Business Man

Colin Chapman first brought the sponsor idea to F1. Today's racing teams depend on sponsors to pump money into developing the expensive speedsters. In return, sponsors put logos all over the cars.

RACING MILESTONES

Lotus stayed in business thanks to many trips to Victory Lane.

- **7 F1 Constructors World Championships:** 1963, 1965, 1968, 1970, 1972, 1973, 1978
- **6 F1 Drivers World Championships:** 1963, 1965, 1968, 1970, 1972, 1978
- **79 Grand Prix victories** for Team Lotus
- **4 Grand Prix victories** for four different **privateers** driving Lotus F1 cars
- **1 Olympic 1992 gold medal** in bicycling
- **1 World Rally Championship** with the Lotus Sunbeam in 1981.

Separate from F1 work, Lotus looks for new designs that gain speed but not weight. The rare 340R Elise (just 340 were built) had no doors and no roof, similar to this prototype sketch.

After 1994, Team Lotus pulled out of Formula One racing—possibly forever, even though rumors still swirl about a return.

asymmetric
    not even or balanced on both sides of a center line

privateers
    in racing, a team operating separately from the carmaker or factory

Fast Fact

Lotus proved its brainpower went beyond cars with its winning lightweight (surprise) **asymmetric** bicycle design.

Racing Ahead

Instead of Formula One cars, Lotus has focused on developing road cars and related track-ready models. The successful Elise prompted a Sport Racer model. The Exige added aerodynamics for faster cornering at the track. Then came the Lotus Circuit Car.

Many Lotus owners join clubs for swapping tips and stories and the opportunity to show off their treasured cars. Some clubs also host races.
Owners must outfit their cars to meet track safety rules.

The Elise Sports Racer rocketed from 0 to 60 miles (97 km) per hour in 4.9 seconds. It nailed 100 miles (160 km) per hour in 13 seconds with a top speed of 150 miles (241 km) per hour.

The spiffed-up 2006 Elise Sport Racer had tighter sports suspension, ultra-light wheels, special tires, and other features ready for club racing. Limited to 199 cars, the model came in red with one white stripe or blue with two white stripes.

In 2005, Lotus designed and built the prototype *Circuit Car* in just 11 weeks. The single-seat track and club racer featured an open cockpit and a supercharged 1.8-liter engine. Lotus announced plans to build only about 100 each year.

Lotus continues to experiment with new designs. The see-through body on the Exposé uses a super-strong plastic material like police riot shields do. What else is ahead for Lotus? Expect something clever, as always—and lightweight, of course.

Fast Fact

The Lotus Circuit Car tests showed the car could rip from 0 to 100 miles (160 km) per hour in 9 seconds. **29**

Glossary

aerodynamic (ahr oh dih NAM ik) – air flows easily over the body for greater speed

asymmetric (ay sah MEH trik) – not even or balanced on both sides of a center line

chassis (CHASS ee) – the frame that supports the body of a vehicle

dies (DIHZ) – shaping devices with holes through which soft metal, plastic, or other material is pressed or drawn

dynamometer (dih nah MOM ih tur) – a tool for measuring a vehicle's power

extruded aluminum (ik STROOD id ah LOO mah nim) – a rust-resistant metal shaped by forcing it through dies or holes

fiberglass (FIY bur glass) –glass strands woven into plastic for added strength

horsepower (HORS pow ur) – a measure of mechanical power; one horsepower equals 550 pounds (885 kg) lifted at one foot (30.5 cm) per second

kit car (KIT KAR) – an unassembled car designed to be built by the owner

light-emitting diode (liht eh MEH ting DIH ohd) – a tiny electronic device that sends out light when energy flows through it

monocoque (MON ah kok) – in vehicles, a body constructed with the frame as a single unit

primer (PRIH mur) – a base paint that seals the surface

privateers (prih vah TEERS) – in racing, a team operating separately from the carmaker or factory

rear-wheel drive (REER WEEL drihv) – the engine drives the rear wheels, pushing the vehicle forward

torque (TORK) – a measure of mechanical strength or force produced by an engine

V-8 (vee AYT) – a motor with eight cylinders set in a V shape; each cylinder has a chamber that burns fuel

Further Reading

Young, Eoin. *Jim Clark and His Most Successful Lotus* Haynes Publications, Inc., 2004.

Taylor, William. *The Lotus Book: The Complete History of Lotus Cars* Coterie Press, Third Ed., 2004.

Pitt, Colin. *The Lotus Book Type 1 to Type 72: The Essential Guide to Historic Lotus Cars.* CP Press, 2005.

Websites

www.formula1.com

www.grouplotus.com

www.historiclotusregister.co.uk

www.lotuscars.com

Index

About the Author

Tracy Nelson Maurer writes nonfiction and fiction books for children, including more than 50 titles for Rourke Publishing LLC. Tracy lives with her husband Mike and two children near Minneapolis, Minnesota.